Actions

for kids age 1-3

By Dayna Martin

e ENGAGE BOOKS

Mailing address
PO BOX 4608
Main Station Terminal
349 West Georgia Street
Vancouver, BC
Canada, V6B 4A1

www.engagebooks.ca

Written & compiled by: Dayna Martin
Edited & designed by: A.R. Roumanis
Photos supplied by: Shutterstock

FIRST EDITION / FIRST PRINTING

LIBRARY AND ARCHIVES CANADA CATALOGUING IN PUBLICATION

Martin, Dayna, 1983–, author
    Actions for kids age 1-3 / written by Dayna Martin ; edited by A.R. Roumanis.

(Engage early readers : children's learning books)
Issued in print and electronic formats.
ISBN 978-1-77226-055-7 (paperback). –
ISBN 978-1-77226-056-4 (bound). –
ISBN 978-1-77226-057-1 (pdf). –
ISBN 978-1-77226-058-8 (epub). –
ISBN 978-1-77226-059-5 (kindle)

1. Human locomotion--Juvenile literature.
I. Roumanis, A. R., editor
II. Title.

QP301.M365 2015   J612.7'6   C2015-903402-7
                                   C2015-903403-5

Actions

for kids age 1-3

Engage Early Readers

Children's Learning Books

by Dayna Martin

ENGAGE BOOKS / VANCOUVER

3

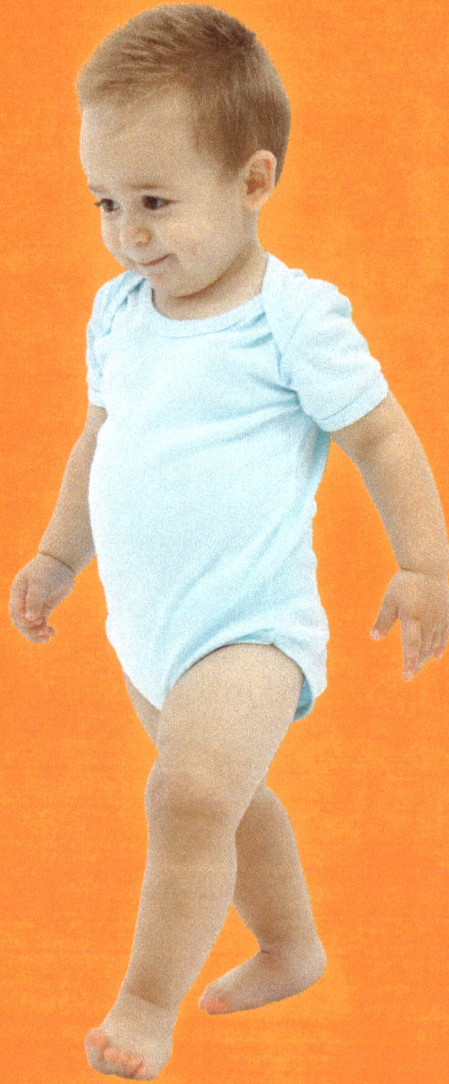

Walk

4

Kiss

5

Climb

6

Clap

7

Ride

Brush

Dive

Swim

11

Kick

12

Eat

Run

14

Hand Stand

15

Hop

Row

17

Pull

18

Pull

19

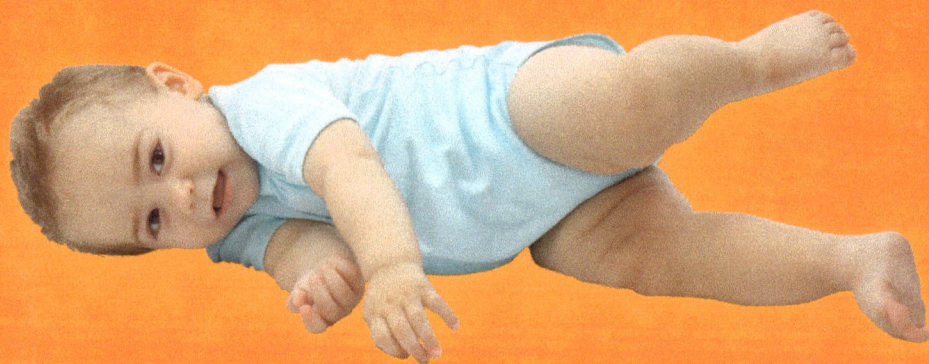

Roll

Balance

Thumbs up

22

Wave

Crawl

Dance

Point

Jump

27

sit

Hit

29

Actions
activity

Do you remember what these actions are called? Can you find **kick**, **clap**, **eat**, **crawl**, **hop**, **wave**, **kiss**, **brush**, and **ride**? Match the names to the actions below.

Answer: kiss

Answer: eat

nswer: hop

Answer: brush

Answer: kick

nswer: wave

Answer: crawl

Answer: ride

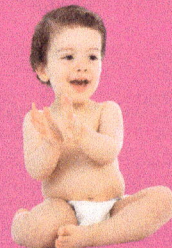

nswer: clap

For other books in this series visit www.engagebooks.ca

age 1-3 Colors for Kids

Yellow Fish
Orange Flower
Purple Eggplant
White Bear
Red Fire Hydrant
Blue Hat
Pink Pig
Green Lego

age 1-3 Opposites for Kids

In
Out
Long
Short
On
Off
Up
Down
Big
Small
Slow
Fast
Front
Back
New
Old

age 1-3 ABCs for Kids

Fox
Lion
Vulture
Tiger
Bear
Rabbit
Dog
Cat

age 1-3 Sizes for Kids

Small
Medium
Large
Small
Medium
Large
Small
Medium
Large
Medium
Large
Small
Small
Medium
Large
Medium
Small
Small
Medium
Large
Large
Medium
Small

age 1-3 Numbers for Kids

4 Raspberries
7 Rubber Ducks
2 Cars
8 Presents
5 Cups
1 Bowl
6 Balloons
3 Pickles

age 1-3 Emotions for Kids

Angry
Joy
Proud
Shy
Brave
Grumpy
Shock
Fear

age 1-3 Shapes for Kids

Starfish
Clock
Leaf
Chalkboard
Door
Rings
Cracker
Pizza

age 1-3 Sounds for Kids

Ribbit
Moo
Vroom
Flush
Clap
Ring
Roar
Cock-a-doodle-doo

age 1-3 Sports for Kids

Badminton
Basketball
Baseball
Volleyball
Soccer
Golf
Tennis

www.ingramcontent.com/pod-product-compliance
Lightning Source LLC
Chambersburg PA
CBHW051310020426
42331CB00020B/3497